THIS MUSIC FROM ANOTHER ROOM

For Pantelis & Julia,

"such is the heart"

yours,

ELIOT CARDINAUX

Eliot Cardinaux

THE BODILY PRESS
Amherst, MA

All poetry by Eliot Cardinaux except where indicated.
First Edition. Copyright © 2024 Eliot Cardinaux

This book is set in Garamond Premier Pro,
Chelsea Market Open, and Source Code Variable.
Book design and layout by Eliot Cardinaux.
eliotcardinaux.com

Cover image: *"Just Man" & Other Works* by Michael Tillyer.
New England Visionary Artists Museum. Northampton, Massachusetts.
Photographed by Heleen Cardinaux. December 30th, 2023.
Inside image: *"Angel"* by Michael Tillyer
All Rights Reserved Copyright © 2024 Michael Tillyer
neva-museum.org

Bodily Press logo designed by Katya Popova.
popova.space

THIS MUSIC FROM ANOTHER ROOM

for Isaac & Zoe

Table of Contents

❧

American Feelings / xi

◆

LETTERS TO APPLETOWN

Refuge / 19
Nine Lives / 21
I love the little loves you make / 22
A Landscape Photograph / 23
100 New Year's Days / 24
Encounter as Imagined / 26
Elskersmål / 27
I Am Wondering / 28
Hudsult / 30

◆

SEATTLE VARIATIONS

The Point / 33
Supersonic Vibration / 34
There's Rainier Tower / 35
Seattle Night Prayer / 36
Seward Park / 37
L'Oursin / 38
On Camano / 39
Iverson Spit / 40

◆

ONGOING EPILOGUE

Ongoing Epilogue / 43
Peter Pan / 44
What the Sun Said / 45
Angel Song / 46
Unluck / 47
Frail Instruments / 49
Poet / 51
Ash / 52

◆

NOTES FROM BIRD LAKE

White horse through the window / 55
Notes from Bird Lake / 56
Doubt / 57
Year House / 59
Power / 60
Distance / 61
To Learn a Little Happiness / 62
Poetry / 63

◆

IN LIGHT OF DARKNESS

1 January 2024 / 67
Search for the New Land / 69
I Dream by the Fire / 70
Duet / 71
Somewhere / 72
Sitting Poem / 73
Grencn / 74

◆

SPEAKING OF A FUTURE

Birthday / 79
Wander / 80
Darling / 81
Speaking of a Future / 82
Modern / 83
Small Grace / 84
Exile / 85
Coming on the Nørrebrogade / 86

◆

Acknowledgments / 91

Notes / 95

About the Author / 99

American Feelings

In January, 2024, I moved to Denmark for a love powerful enough to get me to leave behind my life in the United States. These poems chronicle the time from when we met, till the week after she abruptly ended things. By now, I've come to realize that she couldn't accept me. She saw a truth in me. That I carry around a darkness. One of the signs, she said, is that I approach difficult subjects in my work. But when a friend back home reached out to me in crisis, suicidal, wanting to end his life, she couldn't accept the discomfort it caused me, or my need to respond.

We were at a party. I kept stepping out to smoke, to get away, in panic about my friend; to talk to him. I couldn't handle all the social interaction, loud music, and dancing, in the midst of his long-distance appeals for help. A familiar collision of dissonant realities. My wifi connection was spotty, making it worse. My friend's eventual radio silence that night left me in the dark as to whether he might be alive the next day.

She wanted to take my mind off things ("why don't you dance with my friend?"). I tried my best to stay present. When we later got back to the house, she parked the car and said, quite earnestly, "we need to talk about your smoking."

I explained to her that it was quite a difficult moment to be confronted about my admittedly problematic nicotine addiction. She retorted that my friend was behaving in a way that was "evil," for putting his suicidality on me. That if he was in this position to begin with, he was to blame.

Her choice of words, I thought, must be lost in translation. Did she really view his suffering through such a radically moralistic lens? Writing this now, however, I am reminded of Søren Kierkegaard's treatise, *The Sickness Unto Death*, in which the Danish philosopher rationalizes *ad absurdum* about the immorality of despair.

Perhaps she viewed my friend's abjection through the present-day vestiges of a 19th-Century Danish lens. I may never know.

My own history with depression, anxiety, suicidality, and mental illness has led me here, belonging to a community of likewise struggling individuals — most of them artists — both in the sense of my need for them, and my need to be there for them. Because of my history, doing my best to show up for my friend in his moment of crisis, despite the discomfort it caused me, felt to me like a commitment, in the face of a real, human need. Why did my would-be partner view it as a threat? Why did she stand in the way of it? Why did she deny me her empathy, in the face of such a troubling interaction? I wish, in fact, with some regret, that I had been able to do more, in that moment, to make sure my friend was ok.

When I use the word *able*, it might be that I do not simply refer to an *inability* on my part, to stay emotionally present for my friend, given what he was going through. It might be more complex than that. Though it's hard for me to say. Perhaps I refer to what once constituted my *disability*, under the laws of the U.S. government. I no longer qualify as disabled. So how can I know for sure?

Disability is a legal term, not a medical one, a label that can be given — and taken away — by the state — if not at will, then by a series of quantitative assessments that negate and erase the unseen, often social ramifications of living with such a condition. The precarity of the very validity of one's disability can be — for lack of a better term, though perhaps a befitting one — intensely maddening. It can cause a crisis of identity, especially when one's disability — my perceived depression, my friend's suicidality — is thrown in one's face.

Two years ago, I lost a friend to an overdose. Despite my better inclinations, I had waited too long to make my amends to him, after a difficult emotional break, six months prior to his death. I never got the chance to tell him how much I cared. The recently departed poet and novelist, Paul Auster, writes, in the opening paragraph of his memoir, *Winter Journal*:

You think it will never happen to you, that it cannot happen to you, that you are the only person in the world to whom none of these things will ever happen, and then, one by one, they all begin to happen to you, in the same way they happen to everyone else.

    I understand, on a molecular level, that it was not only my friend, who reached out to me in crisis from overseas, while I was in Denmark, whose vulnerability and mortality I witnessed, the night of the party. It was also me. Paul Celan, a lifelong influence on Paul Auster, wrote of the "congenital darkness" of poetry, an essential darkness that allows for an encounter to take place — an encounter, perhaps not simply with a reader, or interlocutor, but with oneself. I believe I have encountered myself throughout these pages.

    We cannot be simply reduced to symptoms of the societies from which we spring, nor can the functionality of entire societies be fully extrapolated from the behaviors of their individual components. However, with regard to my would-be partner's rejection of the validity of my friend's appeal, and my desire to address it, perhaps it is as simple as the fact that in her experience, there are no apparent, visible, and therefore adequate, valid, or even conceivable reasons for wanting to end one's life. Begging, for instance, is criminalized in Denmark, rendering virtually invisible the reality of absolute poverty in others. The system will take care of it. "The face of evil is always the face of total need," writes William Burroughs. But it doesn't go away because you close your eyes.

    With regard to my own — yes, desperate, implacable, impossible (I very much hesitate to say *American*) — empathy and compassion in relation to my friend, however messy, perhaps I know the meaning of a certain pain because I've been there. To quote another, albeit fictional Dane alongside Kierkegaard, Hamlet's fated quandary, "to be or not to be," remains an essential question, one to be treated with the utmost care and respect, no matter how complicated.

My former teacher, Ocean Vuong, relayed the same to me, when I once approached him in his office during a crisis of my own.

As for my smoking, I've battled addiction all my life. In one week's time, I will be three years sober from alcohol. But if it's not one thing it's another. "You have many good qualities." That was the last thing she ever said to me.

The Russian poet, Joseph Brodsky, once wrote, for a talk given at a conference of writers in exile, held by the Wheatland Foundation in Vienna in December of 1988, after pausing for "those who, quite naturally, didn't make it to this room," a comprehensive list of whom would be impossible to compile, and might make my situation seem quite stable in comparison:

> If there is anything good about exile, it is that it teaches one humility. It accelerates one's drift into isolation, an absolute perspective. Into the condition at which all one is left with is oneself and one's language, with nobody or nothing in between. Exile brings you overnight to where it would normally take a lifetime to go.

Maybe it was her gift — regardless of whether or not it was hers to give — to shirk all responsibility, and leave me stranded in a foreign country with no place to live but this feeling, this leaden substance that I now have to handle with care, and shape into something beautiful.

Eliot Cardinaux
April 1st, 2024

to be lost is a kind of leaving

—Bei Dao

LETTERS TO APPLETOWN

After all these years the snow still smells of apples.

—Osip Mandelstam, "1 January 1924"

Refuge

In darkness
heavy with light I hear
a melody

•

We were moving
segments of a song
up a flight of stairs

•

What lungs
will we use to breathe?

•

An extant dream
we swim in
the swollen river

•

Somewhere
north of the future
there's a place for us

•

A quiet different
from wayside storms

9 Lives

I love the sound of running water in that dim-lit room.
Here, as I sit on a bench and watch the wind blow smoke
across the water, the lighthouse slightly fuzzy in the haze,
no joke I am terrified. & the tree guy buzzes with his saw,
removing the heart of my childhood, in this place that is
more memory than memory. If this is weird, if this is exit
I want to read from it. Like fox kits drinking from a pool.

I love the little loves you make

When there is nothing left
to do

Those insect hotels & arches,
cardhouses of red clay, ceramic
fishes, white-blue cups
with people's names

What we can do
to be of each other
now will thread through null & void
the desire for pity
in every one of us

The world against the world

A Landscape Photograph

I showed my friend
a photo of where you live.
Today I have not had time
to sit & think of those rolling
hills, & the people around me
deserve my attention, coming
up to the counter like waves
on the shore in Appletown.
Tomorrow I will sit & think
of those rolling hills, & soon
be there, not here, I hope, with
a vague uncertainty, as you lie
in bed with a fever I also have.

100 New Year's Days

I wear a lamp as a hat
& now I have your legs.
I am suddenly even taller.
I live in these two worlds.

To be here & watch
the screen light up
& ding with a shirt
you pulled over your face.

Like you I like
a sleepy town,
big drowsy apples,
drooping lids.

Like Mandelstam
I know to kiss
time's troubled,
ancient nodding head

would mean
to seal the old man's lips
& stare into the black-
blue eyes of dragonflies

forever. But to lie in bed & wait
while the heart turns over,
warm still in the nightingale
fever of its grief.

To sing between pieces
of debris your coven song,
the eye in the smile
squinting,

as if you were so small,
& all this in excess of the world,
the lines & the hair,
the flash & grace of it,

were torn from,
sight & sound
(I am only extending the poem)
in the face you make.

Encounter as Imagined

I wanted to be rid of it

When she couldn't
tell if I knew it was her

A slight
dismay of a look
that pierced me

All my imagination
clinging to that exactly

Elskersmål

The skin a hull
over white & iris

Hunger a silt on the ocean
floor

A bird with thin wings flies
through summer

Such is the heart

I Am Wondering

How to dare
interrupt sublimity

•

How raw I feel
& filthy hot

•

Did I leave it
under the table

•

Can I hear you
laugh in my mind
so faintly

•

Forgive me
childlike
futility

•

I'll die too in your arms
if love is the deadly nightshade

•

This wood is so smooth
& white like a bone

Hudsult

Did I spell that right?
Did my language please you?

Summer bird

in our lover tongue

I want

what right now
cannot provide

SEATTLE VARIATIONS

the sky with its light
and the light that almost
since then has recalled
atomic fire
a bit

—Inger Christensen, *Alphabet*

The Point

I'm asking for directions.
You can't hear the smooth
jazz from here. You have to go
into the little green glade to hear
the smooth jazz. Totem poles
& radio-cell towers. The exact
not-knowing. A single thin fir
with no needles below thirty
feet.

Supersonic Vibration

Entering Open Books felt good today.
Especially after overhearing how "the hood
is all for it, the mugshot backfired," & all
the attenuating grumble & laughter from the right-
wing nutcase who invaded the smoker's corner
with his phone at the Point Casino. Why
he was allowed in is beyond the point,
where lightdebris & cavernous words roam
into the night that has yet to fall on this Earth.
This beautiful woman is singing her songs
in the park to no one.

There's Rainier Tower

mushrooming into the sky & around
the corner, gravel that looks like ash.
A psychosis of signage. Each motif is
exchanged in its gruff & smiling currency.
Poetry is, like baseball, a trading card game.

Then there we were, sitting in an Uber in traffic
after the baseball game, & the streets were strangely
quiet. Every once in a while, an ensemble of seagulls
would restlessly send up a glare of sea-cries, clusters
of piano keys jostling up & down under hands of light.

Seattle Night Prayer

The price of the tacos will go unnamed. The alley bodies in prayer & their simple sanity. Love in the eyes of a woman in a lavender shawl, all around her the world & its infinite friendships. The outside seething with complex orations. The earth in its language surrounding a timid brain, a ceiling draped in white plastic wisteria. A candle on every table. I listened to a man rant out his shift, every one of his apologies refused absolutely.

Seward Park

Drove by a wedding the other day.
Am I allowed the inflection as estimate?
The Pacific Northwest is east of the rising
sun, broken in the way I believe I know.

L'Oursin

How cute you looked, counting your miseries before they were upon you. My body stretched out by the lens. Last night caught fire on a liminal level, projecting the fantasy onto the ruins of the earth, a sieve that drew down all vanity, all skullduggery & landscape in equal measure. Is it frightening in cloud city? For this you are nothing but an impasse, light's devoured surface, an attenuating glance. What we see is not what we've gotten once before, but what we could not hold onto long enough to forget.

On Camano

Rufous & Anna's & those little black birds
with the funny eyes

Deadheading spider-like lilies,
finding receipts in the grass

It rains in a slanted
European script

Iverson Spit

Found a faun's head in the washed up trees.
You were looking for something a little more
twisted with a wider base. The little girl you
passed. She was mesmerized by your cane.
& now this is a photograph.

ONGOING EPILOGUE

> Nothing matters except the big lie
> of the personal—the lie in which
> these objects do not believe.
>
> —Jack Spicer, *After Lorca*

Ongoing Epilogue

It must be love.
The poet has surfaced again
& I'm writing to you
from the other side
of loneliness.

There are such unfortunates.
Not one of them is you
& the music tells of
days off their hinges,
swinging open doors.

If only the world would end
tomorrow, unimpeded, loving
you would be. But they
start up the century again
like any other day.

Peter Pan

Two yellow balloons
in quick succession
whisked around each
side of the green bus

& then a third, like a cartoon
tumbleweed, from one bus
to the next, across the yellow
lines & slashes, bumbles

to rest. & there, a white one
resting in front of me;
a slow & easy feeling,
totally incongruent

with the money for the passport,
canceled train, a week for the refund
to come, & all the need! A man exits
the station wearing his bare guitar.

I like how the bus driver honks his horn.
I can't trust myself to wait for the last
second to get on, though he's told me
I've still got time.

What the Sun Said

for Bill Frisell

I go into town to get my poems.
I clean the room. Someone wants me
to ask the big question here, but I feel
I know everything about this place.
I haven't cleaned the room yet.

Angel Song

Imagined & real,
leaking more or less

& the T.V. glaring,
what's your connotation

Broken bridges falling
off the end of a stave
into legato

Time growing easy
when loss is objective

Playing footsie with the vertigo

A spider climbing
Nicolette's long legs

Unluck

*in memoriam
Chick Byrne
& Jody West*

Poems must be written,
must be read

See how the light
like honey
wrestles the dew
& the bruising
continues

Under the left
shoulder

The blades of grass
like a sting in the smile
born of sweat,
the tears
of anything but war

Tonight, the world
dissociates

Under
new names, forceful
rearrangements

Night
licks the forehead off
its fingers

Words
dissolve in the soft
dry mouth

A tragedy as vertigo
breaks against the body
lives
in our hungry ears

I have brushed the leaves
together for the rustle alone

Soft, bright inaction, take me
to where others are lost

Frail Instruments

To chart inane
& other disaster

Stay brave
in the face of a word

Insanity, sensing
the lump & its hunger

Longing
in my throat

To be out here alone
in my animal self

The clarinet, the oud,
that mimic the mouth of the tale

Grief is a portal
to visit the world

The body's chapters
give way

To drink in the night
& its negative darkly

Checkpoint in a field
of sunflowers turning

Walk this prosthetic
landscape

The light is not endemic
nor ceramic

We see our fish there
smiling at the sea

To try & make sense
impossible

The garden makes
a sound

A plane makes
a different sound

A distant crow
kneads the air

Poet

I read his books
& I send him poems

He offers
silence

Truest truist,
let down your general veil

The world is full of monsters,
fantasies

Two sides to a knife
& a sharper edge

O lyric
here comes the froth of me

Ash

Hush now, he's gone.
You lulled some devil to sleep.
& your bemused smile cut through
that cold clear vanity of sound.

NOTES FROM BIRD LAKE

> The dialogue between the near and the far.
> How the center empties as details accumulate.
> How the absent reappears, and the present...
>
> —Michael Palmer, *The Danish Notebook*

White horse through the window

The shiver & shake of my hands

I am such a wave to wash over you

Notes from Bird Lake

When you were falling
noise over mind

•

What
of these misheard arrows
of light in the dark
of the mind, this
placelessness

To whom do I refer

•

No one
    can force me to talk

Trees, too
    have the right to remain
        silent

That one
    standing alone in a field,
        a criminal

Doubt

The wind estranged, entangled
in odious wood

Death's leaves then ignited —
aimless fury
how are we satisfied

•

The wind encircling the space
could well feed flames

To envy the Buddha's strength,
fight with the warmth of the house

•

A spider went under her sleeve.
She lends her breath to the music.
We've eaten a lot of apples,
come to another bear's cave

•

There's that refrain again

If fears were allowed to live
there would be rhetoric to control it

This music
from another room

Till morning then in a newer town
all this strangeness in the dark

Year House

What kind of house is this

Is it open
to the light inside
for any reason

Or
    what

Other than love,
there are these instruments,
the light of a blank page,

The scribble of material
felt by the hands

Power

We talked about that earth,
a dark place, a railroad yard.

He apologized & accused you.
You brought it out in him.

A trip to the balcony, hanging
over our lives in negative.

A single smoke, essential
solitude; to scribble a few lines

while he crumbled macaroons
over shaved apples, talking

so much he whipped
the cream into butter.

Distance

This place,
your past in it,
flowing out of a cracked pane

(another power,
curling around you like sleep,
eyes paralyzed)

•

I can think of many answers,
but why does the birch
know everything?

•

At night, deserted,
I can feel myself a town,
a teacher, eyes closed
between the mark &
the feeling, ascribed
a hesitant dark for my
mutinous humility. I think of
the drum, a pen, the pen,
a drum, & the drum,
a raised hair.

To Learn a Little Happiness

I've been thinking about how the darkness of the poem pulls me away. Under the birch tree, an abyss lights up. The firmament locked in suspension. Cigarettes, only an excuse. To be with the dark, clutching my heart. To learn a little happiness.

Poetry

Another language
spoken around us

Certain specific
words transcribe

Meaning nothing
known you learn

Between a country
& its landscape

Signs of here
& nowhere

IN LIGHT OF DARKNESS

He who walks on his head, ladies and gentlemen—
he who walks on his head, has the sky
beneath himself as an abyss.

—Paul Celan, *The Meridian*

1 January 2024

for Ewa Chrusciel

A clapper stick,
broad church walls,
white with a gag
of leather

Folk angel, imbecile angel

Not like the drunken
Romani bear, dear Ewa,
in the sense of light

Small taste
of weakness from the golden
cup of its wings

To straddle
between two worlds
a century, the span
between these years,
a literary life & that
of a circus bear

The queen & king
adjusting the pieces,
a cat goes here, a mouse goes there

& the birds
startled from their reedy
melody, the fright
of a bow-stricken string
in Bach's
penultimate fugue

Search for the New Land

Thick fog, as if the air were
snow. Dark purple, guttural cry
of the blood, tufts of *gyvel* stick
up from the quiet; spikes of sugar.

As the dark sky envelops this
interim, my fighting for & against
its warmth, a blank page, daring me
to walk outside, will answer.

I Dream by the Fire

after Osip Mandelstam

Fantastical processes lining the insides of beasts, where theory gives way to imagination. Horns freezing out of liquids slowly injected into form, as darkness might dream of a flame. Balkan music leans into inevitable sorrow. Life, in its invitation, an environment surrounding a species held under a magnifying glass, permitted at last to die. Your obsession with naturalists. The warbling of birdsong, attuned, and yet, like a radio in a fast-moving car, always in danger of losing a signal. The dreamer remembers the dream, but cannot recall it.

Duet

after Iliassa Sequin

Your master neither master nor
anonymous
in synonym with hers.

Fierce form in the breakers.
The land is not swept away.

That part of myself that mostly
fears itself, & the breath that opens
onto the moon in a ray of clouds.

That the outside is in, & the inside out,
& so, below, the depths are also lighted.

Somewhere

Nowhere in the wind
the one in your room
coughs non-descriptly
against the lashing of
the branches, rattle of
the stove, like folklore.

Venture to a corner
under the overhang
to smoke & watch
the bamboo dance
with good humor
against the buffeting wind.

You can hear a dog barking
thinking it stranded
outside in the dark
as you lock the car
walking back to the house against
the menace of the wind.

Sitting Poem

A kestrel hovers
over the field out back.
Scotch broom chokes
the landscape.

I should pull one up every day.
A bright-green, rooted
tumbleweed.

Bright green! In the middle of winter!

Bamboo hisses in the wind
with the clatter of birds.
I am working
up to an excess.

See how it dances? Waving
like a child against the blue.
Goodbye, bamboo!

Grenen

*to the memory of Paul Celan,
& the martyrs in Rafah*

Beached heart there,
a branch of shadow
up from the sand.

No music,
no
puppet-string.

•

I did not heed my warning,
actor, coughing blood.

Diary, *Concerto Al-Quds*—
while you deliberate

(*Rygning skader
dine lunger*)

Höss on-screen behind the wall
glimpses his factory

from which no goods
(no good) can come

other than stolen
(stolen good)

& the verb
to concentrate

SPEAKING OF A FUTURE

As it is we never emerge from the dance

—Osip Mandelstam, *Tristia*

Birthday

The smell of sleep as sun
slants over the water

(You are waking)

I wash the smoke
off my hands

(When you walk in
a room full of people)

I have no word to call
the whistle of your name

Wander

Little doubt-sprite,
hover at the threshold of snow

Last night I wrestled
phantoms into forms of return

Tried not to whisper panic
into my sleeping
lover's ear

Emptied contents of a letter
onto the kitchen table

As I shut the door
I know by morning
you will return

Darling

A birch grows fast. Meaning
perpendicular, circumference.

To burn in a field of action, black
as protest, free as no one. The way

the way is misty, a distant purpose.
Unkindness, a barn behind it, flit-

tering of grief among the voices.
What are they saying? The words

are not important. How long
for the birch to grow?

Speaking of a Future

We were driving up north
to a tooth of land that lay
in a North Sea cavity. You asked me to take away
your fear. How many years has it been,
old snow? How many broken
legs on the garden's
conscience?

Had we not spoken of the lone cow
howling through the cruelty of the hills
I might never have echoed how
I could hear your eyelashes moving
against the skin of my cheek,
a butterfly's wings.

Modern

Enough to spare us
the legato braid
of a double loss

Signaling anonymous
particulars. No longer

Among the living,
who still walks this earth?

No grim smile, no
dactyl. I am driven insane
by my will to live. Not to be
your responsibility. Why am I still
when the world is moving
around me, cars in the road,
a whirlwind?

Small Grace

It took the right words to hear
the bird singing in your chest

A transparent song to say
I love you

Learned it from memory
(maybe crazy's not the word)

When the walls shout
& birds fall still

It can happen to anyone taken
at their word

The dream & the doing fall
still while the heart is shouting

Exile

The gift of isolation
a muted number,
measure despite none.

Coming on
the Nørrebrogade

Nightly, the wind
blows backwards. Book

laid open, empty, burning
in newness. No-moon

whose shadow flaps down
like a piece of cellophane.

Will you be my friend?
A man on a bike, now,

I am red-nosed
strictly from the cold.

Have you heard of a place
to live? I hear I've been

so sweet. But how
many steps away

from this or into it?
Things will make sense, you

fumble around in the dark
for long enough.

Look at me, indignant
on the train. An impossible

homeland in my ears
to stay my anxious roving

eyes. I will find
the address he gave me.

A living stranger cocks
her head, a kind of gnosis

as we disembark. To witness
all the ugly beauty in this

world. Take satisfaction
from my peace of mind.

I will relish a moment
alone with my hurt.

A familiar name glares
out from a street sign.

Its meaning opens
onto the city.

Words on a darkened window.
February dances in its ring.

Winter has become a sail,
a buffeting, red, red rose.

A new neighbor in crisis
smoking out the window,

I'll hold fast to the skeleton
song of transparent spring.

Acknowledgments

My sincere thanks to the editors of the following journals in which these poems first appeared.

"The Point" in *Cruel Garters*.

"Seattle Night Prayer," "Seward Park," and "*L'Oursin*" in *Broken Lens Journal*.

"Ongoing Epilogue" in *Red Door*.

"Unluck" and "Frail Instruments" in *Spirit Duplicator*.

"Year House" and "Poetry" in *Meat for Tea*.

A segment of "Coming on the Nørrebrogade" as "Contronym" in *Bennington Review*.

Poetry in this collection also appeared in the following chapbooks by the author, published by The Bodily Press: *Letters to Appletown* (2023); *Ongoing Epilogue* (2023); *Notes from Bird Lake* (2023); *Tournesol* (2024); and *In Light of Darkness* (2024).

The poems "White horse through the window," "Notes from Bird Lake," and "Doubt" also appear on the album *Imminence* (self-released, 2024) with Gary Fieldman on percussion, and the author on piano. The album was co-produced by the musicians, with Warren Amerman. My thanks to Gary and Warren for inviting the poetry in.

A loving thank you to Michael Tillyer for the generous use of his marvelous artworks that appear on the cover and title page.

I am deeply grateful to Ivy Schweitzer, for the generosity of her readership and editing of this collection, as well as for her friendship, support, and encouragement.

A heartfelt thank you to Rebecca Faulkner for her readership, essential friendship, and solidarity, and for encouraging me to expand my essay "American Feelings" and include it as a foreword.

Deep gratitude to Tom Snarsky for being a lucid first reader of these poems from the outset.

A sincere thank you to Shana Bulhan for their readership, for their kindness in the face of much vulnerability, and for encouraging my questions surrounding notions of disability as they appear in the foreword.

A very warm thank you to Michael Tillyer and Susan Foley at the New England Visionary Artists Museum for providing a space for this work to grow, and to Peter Gizzi, Patrick Pritchett, Isaac Luxon, Gary Fieldman, Caleb Schmale, and Will McEvoy, for reading and performing with me there.

A very kind thank you to Nat Herold, Shannon Ramsey, Sean Norton, and the rest of the staff at Amherst Books for providing an invaluable sense of belonging and community, on both sides of the ocean from here to here.

A very special thank you to Asger Thomsen, Carolyn Goodwin, Taus Bregnhøj-Olesen, Michaela Turcerová, Liv Blazejewicz, Ben Rodney, Simon Forchhammer, Kresten Osgood, Elizabeth Torres, Jesper Løvdal, Hein Westgaard, Margaux Oswald, Thomas Pogue, Ulla Lundsgart, Liss Hansen, and Niels Vincentz, for their friendship in Denmark.

A deep bow to Peter Gizzi and Ocean Vuong for the lasting impact of their mentorship.

A special thank you to Jo Ianni for our ongoingly illuminating dialogue, and to Adrian Lürssen for seeing so much into these often open forms.

A very warm thank you to Carole d'Inverno and Bill Frisell for their correspondence.

A very kind thank you to Paul and Ange Dutton for the worthwhile excuse to visit Seattle, to Suzy and Jeff Dutton for the sojourn on Camano, and to Menno van Wijk for his hospitality.

Profound love and gratitude to Jade Welch, with whom I remain gratefully entangled.

A very real thank you to Flin van Hemmen, Bram Kincheloe, Ryan Snow, Ryan Blotnick, Isaac Luxon, Sammy Lê, Sharonee Dasgupta, and Katya Popova, for getting stuck in the mud with me.

Finally, a heartfelt thank you to my ever-present family.

Notes

In the foreword, "American Feelings," the Paul Auster quotation is from *Winter Journal* (McClelland and Stewart, 2012). The Paul Celan quotation is from *The Meridian: Final Version—Drafts—Materials*, Pierre Joris, translator; Bernhard Böschenstein and Heino Schmull, editors (Stanford University Press, 2011). The William S. Burroughs quotation is from *Naked Lunch* (Grove Press, 2013). The Joseph Brodsky quotation is distilled from several unjoined paragraphs in his essay, "The Condition We Call Exile, or Acorns Aweigh," collected in *On Grief and Reason: Essays* (FSG, 2020). Søren Kierkegaard's *The Sickness Unto Death* is available through Penguin Books (1989).

The epigraph at the beginning of this collection is from Bei Dao's poem "Requiem," collected in *Unlock*, Eliot Weinberger and Iona Man-Cheong, translators (New Directions, 2000).

The epigraphs at the beginning of each section of this collection are taken respectively from the following books: *The Selected Poems of Osip Mandelstam* (both Mandelstam quotations), translated by Clarence Brown and W.S. Merwin (NYRB, 2004); Inger Christensen's *Alphabet*, translated by Susanna Nied (New Directions, 2001); Jack Spicer's *After Lorca*, collected in *My Vocabulary Did This to Me: The Collected Poetry of Jack Spicer*, edited by Peter Gizzi and Kevin Killian (Wesleyan University Press, 2010); Michael Palmer's *The Danish Notebook* (Nightboat Books, 2023 Reissue); and Paul Celan's *Meridian* (Stanford) (in reference to Georg Büchner's *Lenz*).

In the poem "Refuge," the line "north of the future" is borrowed from a poem in Paul Celan's *Atemwende* (*Breathturn*), as translated by Pierre Joris, and collected in *Breathturn into Timestead: The Collected Later Poetry* (FSG, 2014).

"100 New Year's Days" contains lines collaged from Osip Mandelstam's poems "1 January 1924," and "The clock-cricket singing," as translated by Clarence Brown and W.S. Merwin, in *The Selected Poems of Osip Mandelstam* (NYRB).

The title *"Elskersmål"* is a Danish neologism, meaning "Lover-tongue" (derived from *"modersmål,"* or "mother tongue"). The term derives from its English usage in an essay by Pierre Joris, titled, "The case of the missing 'M,'" collected in his volume, *A Nomad Poetics* (Wesleyan University Press, 2003). My poem employs Danish-English transliterations, such as "summer bird" (*"sommerfugl,"* i.e. "butterfly"), as well as loose, homophonic translations such as "hull"/ "silt" (*"hud"*/ *"sult,"* literally "skin"/ "hunger"). See, also, the title and the poem, *"Hudsult."*

In "Supersonic Vibration," "Open Books" refers to a poetry bookshop in Seattle, WA.

In the poem "Ongoing Epilogue," the lines "It must be love. / The poet has surfaced again" derive from a letter in Jack Spicer's *After Lorca*, collected in *My Vocabulary Did This to Me* (Wesleyan). The lines "if only the world would end / tomorrow, unimpeded, loving / you would be" derive from one of Franz Kafka's *Letters to Milena* (Knopf Doubleday, 2015).

"Ash" is titled after an album by the Mat Maneri Quartet (Sunnyside, 2023).

"Angel Song" is titled after an album by trumpeter/composer Kenny Wheeler (ECM, 1997). "Nicolette" is the title of the opening track.

"What the Sun Said" is titled after a song by guitarist John Fahey, from his album *The Dance of Death & Other Plantation Favorites* (Takoma, 1965/Concord, 1999 CD Reissue).

"Search for the New Land" is titled after an album by trumpeter/composer Lee Morgan (Blue Note, 1966). *"Gyvel"* is the Danish name for Scotch broom, an invasive species of plant that lives on the hillside in Jutland.

"I Dream by the Fire" derives material from Osip Mandelstam's *Journey to Armenia* (NYRB, 2018).

"Duet" is titled after Iliassa Sequin's posthumous chapbook of letters to André du Bouchet, *Duets* (Distance No Object, 2023).

The title "Grenen" refers to the beach at the northernmost tip of Denmark, in Skagen. The poem describes a Nazi bunker, one of several left there standing, remnants of the Second World War. *Concerto Al-Quds* is the title of a book of poetry by the Syrian poet Adonis, strongly critiquing monotheism. *"Al-Quds"* is the Arabic name for Jerusalem. The name "Höss" refers to Rudolf Höss, the Nazi commandant in charge of Auschwitz III, specifically as he is portrayed in the film, *The Zone of Interest*, directed by Jonathan Glazer. The phrase *"Rygning skader / dine lunger"* is a Danish warning on a cigarette label. The Danish tobacco companies are required by law to feature such a warning, alongside photographic depictions of the agonies caused by long-term smoking addiction.

"Coming on the Nørrebrogade" makes use of ideas discussed in Patrick Pritchett's essay, "How to Write Poetry After Auschwitz: The Burnt Book of Michael Palmer," collected in *Make it Broken: Toward a Poetics of Late Modernism* (Black Square Editions, 2025). The poem is titled after "Coming on the Hudson," a piece by pianist/composer Thelonious Monk, which appears as a bonus track on his album *Criss Cross* (Columbia, 1963/2003 CD Reissue). "Nørrebrogade" is a main street in Nørrebro, a district of Copenhagen, Denmark.

About the Author

ELIOT CARDINAUX is a poet, pianist, composer, and translator working at the edges of the lyric and improvised music. The author of *On the Long Blue Night* (Dos Madres, 2023), and the trio of *Quiet Labor*, *Toy Elegy*, and *This Music From Another Room* (Bodily Press, 2024), as well as numerous chapbooks, Cardinaux has also produced and appeared on over a dozen albums of original music, including *American Thicket* (Loyal Label, 2016); *Out of Our Systems* and *Pavane* (Bodily Press, 2022); and most recently *Imminence* (self-released, 2024) with American percussionist Gary Fieldman. He holds a bachelor's degree in contemporary improvisation from The New England Conservatory of Music, and an MFA in creative writing, with a focus on poetry, from the University of Massachusetts in Amherst. Eliot's poems and translations have appeared in journals such as *California Quarterly*, *Tupelo Quarterly*, *Meridian*, *Jacket2*, *The Arts Fuse*, *Bennington Review*, *Solstice*, and *Spoon River Poetry Review*. At present, he co-leads an American trio with bassist Will McEvoy and drummer Max Goldman, works in a duo with Gary Fieldman, leads his own Danish Quartet, and is a member of the European-based free-improvisation ensemble, Our Hearts as Thieves. He has appeared, in various settings, with musicians such as Kresten Osgood, Mat Maneri, Randy Peterson, Thomas Morgan, Asger Thomsen, Ryan Blotnick, Eivind Opsvik, Niels Vincentz, Taus Bregnhøj-Olesen, Isaac Luxon, Flin van Hemmen, and Mia Dyberg. He performs throughout Europe and the Northeast United States. He has taught literature and writing at UMass Amherst, and works as a bookseller at Amherst Books. He is the sole founder and editor of The Bodily Press.

Author photograph by poet Denver Butson • denverbutson.com

THE BODILY PRESS
bodilypress.bandcamp.com